Animal Diaries
Life Cycles

A Bird's Life

by
Ellen Lawrence

Consultants:

Anne Hobbs
Public Information Specialist
Cornell Lab of Ornithology, Cornell University, Ithaca, New York

Kimberly Brenneman, PhD
National Institute for Early Education Research, Rutgers University, New Brunswick, New Jersey

BEARPORT
PUBLISHING

New York, New York

Credits

Cover, © Stubblefield Photography/Shutterstock and © Anne Kitzman/Shutterstock; 3, © Steve Russell Smith Photos/
Shutterstock; 4T, © Richard Susanto/Shutterstock; 4–5, © Joshua Haviv/Shutterstock; 5, © Steve Byland/Shutterstock; 6, ©
Ron Rowan Photography/Shutterstock; 7, © Minden Pictures/Superstock; 8T, © topten22photo/Shutterstock; 8M, © S&D&K
Maslowski/FLPA; 8B, © Gary Carter/Visuals Unlimited/Corbis; 9, © Anne Kitzman/Shutterstock; 11, © Parsons1/Wikipedia
Creative Commons; 12 (Left to Right), © Ioannis Pantzi/Shutterstock; © Irin-K/Shutterstock; © Sarah2/Shutterstock; © ajt/
Shutterstock; 12–13, © Minden Pictures/Superstock; 14, © Doug Lemke/Shutterstock; 14–15, © Sari O'Neal/Shutterstock; 16,
© Carla Kishinami; 17, © Imagebroker/FLPA; 18, © John Kunze; 19, © Marie Read/Photoshot.com; 21L, © R. Marnold/Istock;
21R, © Brian Lasenby/Shutterstock; 22TL, © Perutskyi Petro/Shutterstock; 22TR, © Ekaterina Lin/Shutterstock; 22C, © Anest/
Shutterstock; 22BL, © HamsterMan/Shutterstock; 22BR, © Sommai/Shutterstock; 23TL, © topten22photo/Shutterstock; 23TC, ©
imagebroker.net/Superstock; 23TR, © Parsons1/Wikipedia Creative Commons; 23BL, © Gala Kan/Shutterstock; 23BC, © Steve
Byland/Shutterstock; 23BR, © Anne Kitzman/Shutterstock; 24BL, © R. Marnold/Istock; 24BR, © Brian Lasenby/Shutterstock.

Publisher: Kenn Goin
Editorial Director: Adam Siegel
Creative Director: Spencer Brinker
Design: Alix Wood
Editor: Mark J. Sachner
Photo Researcher: Ruby Tuesday Books Ltd

Library of Congress Cataloging-in-Publication Data

Lawrence, Ellen, 1967-
  A bird's life / by Ellen Lawrence.
     p. cm. — (Animal diaries: life cycles)
  Includes bibliographical references and index.
  ISBN 978-1-61772-595-1 (library binding) — ISBN 1-61772-595-1 (library binding)
  1. Birds—Life cycles—Juvenile literature. I. Title.
  QL676.2.L39 2013
  598.156—dc23
                          2012012472

For more information, write to Bearport Publishing Company, Inc., 45 West 21st Street, Suite 3B,
New York, New York 10010. Printed in the United States of America.

10 9 8 7 6 5 4 3 2 1

Contents

New Neighbors

Today, I spotted two birds flying from tree to tree in our backyard.

They were a male and a female northern cardinal.

My dad said the birds have **mated** because it's spring.

Now they are looking for a place to build a **nest** so the female can lay her eggs.

Max

A male northern cardinal has bright red feathers. A female is brown with some red feathers. The birds have orange beaks and a crest of feathers on top of their heads.

In what ways do the male and female cardinal look alike? How are they different?

female northern cardinal

male northern cardinal

crest

beak

feathers

5

Date: March 31

Nest Building

The female cardinal is building a nest in a tree in our backyard.

It looks like a little bowl made from twigs.

The male bird looks for twigs and then carries them back to the female.

She carefully adds each twig to the nest using her beak and feet.

Today, I saw the female collecting soft, dry grass to put inside the nest.

male northern cardinal

6

It takes a male and female cardinal between three and nine days to build a nest.

female northern cardinal

twig

nest

Date: _April 3_____

The Eggs Are Here

To get a close-up view of the nest, I watch it through my **binoculars**.

The female bird has laid three eggs in the nest.

She sits on them so that they don't get cold.

The **chicks** inside the eggs need to be kept warm to help them grow.

The female will sit on the eggs until they **hatch**.

These northern cardinal eggs are life-size.

a female sitting in a nest

8

Date: April 15

The Chicks Hatch

The female cardinal has been sitting on her eggs for 12 days.

The male bird has been bringing her food.

This morning, three chicks hatched from the eggs!

The chicks' eyes are closed, so they cannot see.

The babies have no feathers—just a little gray fluff.

A newly hatched cardinal chick cannot fly or walk. It can't even stand up!

Imagine one of your friends has never seen a new chick. Describe what the bird looks like to your friend.

northern cardinal chick

egg that hasn't hatched yet

Date: April 21

Three Hungry Chicks

The cardinal chicks are now six days old.

Their eyes have opened, and feathers are sprouting from their little bodies.

The hungry chicks squawk and beg for food.

The parent birds catch **insects** for the chicks and bring them to the nest.

They drop the insects into the babies' wide-open mouths.

The chicks eat spiders and insects such as these.

caterpillar

fly

barn funnel weaver spider

grasshopper

a father cardinal feeding a chick

chick

Adult northern cardinals sometimes eat insects, but they mainly eat seeds and fruit, such as blackberries.

Date: April 23

Chicks in Danger!

Many animals hunt and eat cardinals.

Today, I heard a noise in the yard that sounded like *shriek, shriek!*

The cardinals were telling each other that there was danger.

A cat was near their nest.

The parent birds flew at the cat to scare it away.

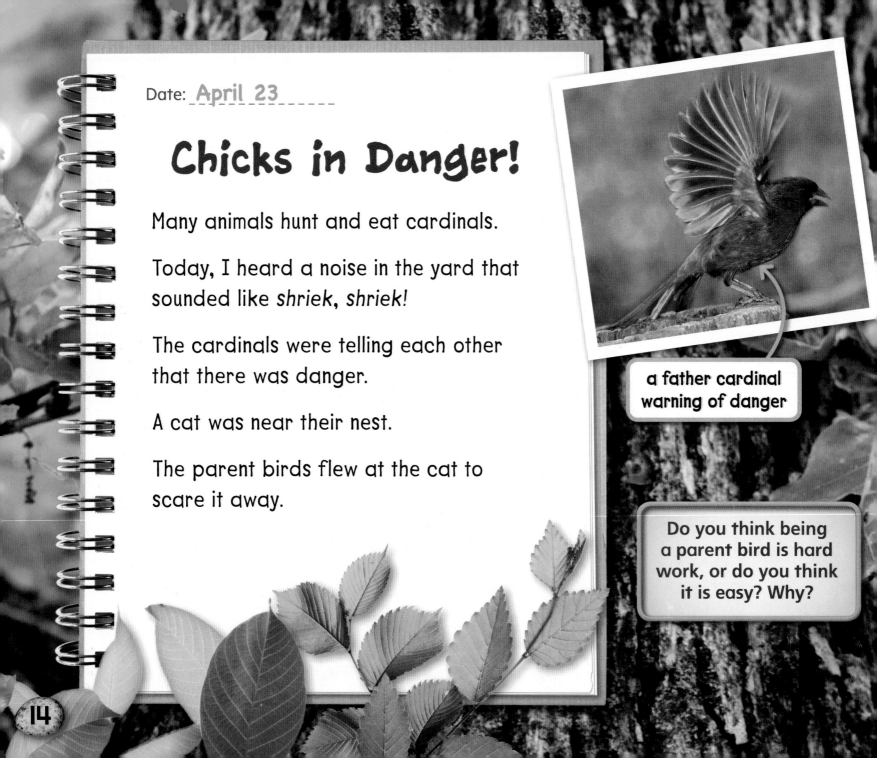

a father cardinal warning of danger

Do you think being a parent bird is hard work, or do you think it is easy? Why?

Pet cats and large
birds such as owls eat adult
northern cardinals and their
chicks. Snakes, squirrels, and
chipmunks eat cardinal
eggs and chicks.

15

Date: April 27

An Amazing Day

The 12-day-old chicks are now flapping their wings and hopping around the nest.

Today, one of the chicks climbed onto the edge of the nest.

It flapped its little wings—and then it jumped!

The chick flew from the nest and landed on a branch next to its mother.

Soon, all three chicks were flying around the yard.

a chick getting ready to leave its nest

12-day-old chick

During the babies' first flight, parent birds cheer on their chicks with chirps and calls.

Date: May 27

Growing Up

The chicks are now six weeks old.

They know how to find insects to eat, but they still beg for food from their father.

They show him they want to be fed by fluttering their wings.

The mother bird no longer feeds the chicks.

She is too busy building a new nest so that she can lay more eggs.

a mother cardinal collecting grass for a nest

A pair of cardinals will raise two or three groups of chicks each year.

Feathered Friends

I've been watching the cardinal chicks all summer.

Now they are growing red and brown feathers.

Soon the young birds will fly off to look for new places to live.

By spring, they will be adults and ready to raise their own chicks.

Northern cardinals become adults when they are about one year old. They usually live between 4 and 13 years.

Look at the two young
cardinals in these pictures.
Which one do you think is a
male and which is a female?

(The answer is on page 24.)

Science Lab

Be a Bird Scientist

Find out what foods birds like to eat best.

First, find a place where there are lots of birds.

It could be your backyard or a park.

Then put different bird foods on a tray.

Place the tray where you see birds, and sit quietly nearby for 30 minutes.

In a notebook, keep a record of how many birds try each food.

Your record could look like this.

Bird food	Number of birds
sunflower seeds	l l l l
corn	l l l l l l l
chopped-up fruit	l
breadcrumbs	
peanuts	

Which food did the birds like best?

Here are some ideas for bird foods.

sunflower seeds

corn

chopped-up fruit

breadcrumbs

peanuts

Borrow a bird book from the library. Try to find pictures of the birds that visited your food.

Science Words

binoculars (buh-NOK-yuh-lurz) a tool for seeing a close-up view of things that are far away

chicks (CHIKSS) baby birds

hatch (HACH) to break out of an egg

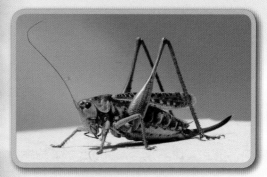

insects (IN-sekts) small animals that have six legs, two antennas, a hard covering called an exoskeleton, and three main body parts

mated (MAYT-id) came together in order to have young

nest (NEST) a home built by birds where they lay their eggs and raise their chicks

Index

Read More

Lundgren, Julie. *Chickens (Life Cycles)*. Vero Beach, FL: Rourke (2011).

Scrace, Carolyn. *Egg to Bird (Cycles of Life)*. New York: Scholastic (2002).

Zollman, Pam. *A Chick Grows Up*. New York: Scholastic (2005).

Learn More Online

To learn more about birds, visit **www.bearportpublishing.com/AnimalDiaries**

Answers

Here is the answer to the question on page 21.

young female
northern cardinal

young male
northern cardinal

About the Author

Ellen Lawrence lives in the United Kingdom. Her favorite books to write are those about animals. In fact, the first book Ellen bought for herself, when she was six years old, was the story of a gorilla named Patty Cake that was born in New York's Central Park Zoo.